(About *The Gathering Wave*)
"Some of the richest examples of haiku art I have seen...."
Robert Beum (Prairie Schooner)

"A few years from now collectors will be looking for this book...."
The Chicago Tribune

"Some of the best ever written...."
Tom McGrath (TheNational Guardian)

(About *A Garden of Sound*)
"What Rilke says of Orpheus is also true of Alvaro, he sets up a tall tree in our ears...."
John Minczeski

"Cardona-Hine is one of the strongest lyric poets at work today."
Gene Frumkin

"*Claridades* is a collection of eclectic, profound, and more than anything, diaphanous poems.
Marjorie Agosín

"Cardona-Hine writes poetry, and prose, creates beautiful paintings, composes music, is politically to the Left, and likes to smoke a good cigar."
Gary L. Brower, *Malpais Review*

Previous books by the author:

Romance de Agapito Cascante
The Gathering Wave
The Flesh of Utopia
Menashtash
Agapito
Words on Paper
Spain, Let This Cup Pass from Me (Trans. of Vallejo)
Two Elegies
The Half-Eaten Angel
Miss O'Keeffe
Four Poems About Sparrows
A History of Light
Thirteen Tangos for Stravinsky
Spring Has Come
Cucarachananda
Orpheus Home
Frankenstein in Love
Sucursal de Estrella
Claridades
The Curvature of the Earth
The Recumbent Galaxy
Little Songs to Sing While Singing
The Pocket Machado
Arabesque
The Song Less/on
Phantom Buddha

MEMORY'S VILLAGE

Poems from the north of New Mexico

Alvaro Cardona-Hine

Alba Books Press

Cover photo by Jeane George Weigel
highroadartist.com

Paperback ISBN 978-0615900605

Email: support@cardonahinegallery.com

For Barbara, who lives higher up the mountain.

These poems deal with life in a small Hispanic town in the mountains of northern New Mexico. Eight thousand feet altitude… poverty… a culture in part destroyed by over one hundred years of Anglo domination. My wife and I first came for an extended visit of two months. We rented a three-room adobe dwelling heated only by the cooking stove. The first part of this book, The Visit, was written then. A year later we returned to stay, and bought a house in the village. The poems of Part Two, The Stay, are the result of a commitment to the silence of a silent world and the light that burns the land.

ACH

PART ONE

the visit

<u>one</u>

come visit

I'll show you
a fire engine rusting
in the yard
and the rust
of the mountains
in the sky

<u>two</u>

a candle in the dining room
a kerosene lamp in the bedroom
everything else
utter darkness

three

I want to buy
the abandoned house
behind the mass
of wild roses

but inside it
I know
your naked body
would turn
to perfume

four

two hours before dawn

the tea
tastes bitter

<u>five</u>

snowflakes

loose stars

<u>six</u>

you brought me
two jars of honey

one I opened
and one I kept
for when I needed
more than two jars
of honey

seven

in the midst
of squalor
I dream
that we open up
our bodies
and find in them
our hearts

eight

when I was young
I thought I had
everything

and I did

now all I have is
my breath and
my breath is dancing
out of reach

nine

above Truchas
in meadows
shorn of wheat
the snow
and the horses
invent a December
of patience

ten

today
at the cemetery
the wind
and the snow
are quarreling
over which graves
to bury

eleven

the sun
on the windowsill
wants to cool its wings
on a geranium

twelve

winter

the dogs are barking
at the fog

thirteen

four dandelions

a yellow moth

otherwise the forest
clad in white

fourteen

how great
for this land
of the sky
to let drunk
light
drive home
without
a license

fifteen

the fire
in its narrow
stove coffin
knocks on the
cast-iron
wall
to let us know
how warm
its dying
makes us

sixteen

in the brook
the water
wild
with neither life
nor death

seventeen

when one reads
Po Chu-I
it's as if the wind
at the door
were a friend
that was there also
when everything
calms down

eighteen

the two have just
emerged from night
when the sun renders
the flanks of the magpie
iridescent

nineteen

in the ditch
an animal
for whom the snow
is dancing
as if death
was going to melt
in its mouth

twenty

after the storm
Truchas Peak and its brothers
stand up against the sky
not only with the greatest clarity
but with small conflagrations
which the wind invents
out of loose snow

twenty-one

the little
being taught here

men with heavy wives
smoke from the dump
curling past the cemetery

a raven
forwarding shadow
to its shadow

twenty-two

the garlic sprouts

a bird passes high
over the upturned mouth
of a field

its wing
a busy priest
aspersing wine

twenty-three

each piece of mica
in this immensity
allows
whatever moon
is up
to alight
on its flanks

twenty-four

from the depths
of the forest
comes the breath
with which the flowers
sing

children who have found
where the wine is kept

twenty-five

night
in the tenebrous
whale
of the sky

loony rodents
in its hold

<u>twenty-six</u>

one or two
small potatoes
dance
in your mouth
and my mouth
letting off
steam

<u>twenty-seven</u>

Sunday
you offer me
salad and bread

you bring out the wine

you moisten my lips
with the perfect after-taste
of your lips

twenty-eight

cow dung
on the side streets
in the alleys
and where it merges
with horseshit
to become this as yet
unlimited promise
of scarabs
and hyacinths

twenty-nine

I am sure
you can tell
by the look
on my face
that I have
finally met
the man who sells
honey

thirty

Delfino
our landlord
brings the mail over
with his delicate
smile

or he brings
fresh bread
that same
delicate smile
has baked

thirty-one

Eliseo
chops wood
for six hours

illiterate
and wonderful

<u>thirty-two</u>

on the shortest day
of the year
the light
is so abundant
that only a memory
can smile
the way it does

look
it escapes
and is gone
and it has never
been

thirty-three

it is afternoon
before we hear
the same rooster
twice

evening
before we know
that was all there was
to this village
Sunday

thirty-four

the acequia
is frozen over
but underneath
they're getting away
with our liquid assets

thirty-five

the poplars live
six months
with hardly a sparrow
to their name

then
each autumn
they win
the lottery

thirty-six

Christmas Eve

love and longing
invent
once again
a world
of four children

thirty-seven

from cliffs
from haze and distance
pastures and peaks
nothing comes to interrupt
this romping of my dog
in the field Delfino
wants to sell me

thirty-eight

three horses
loose on the road

one of them wants
into the cemetery
where the flowers
are plastic

thirty-nine

the old men here
creep daily
along the successful
edge of their shadows

all else
surely
past their eyes

forty

near the precipice
a deer's bygone
mandible
nibbles windy grass

forty-one

the thirty-six acres
of Delfino's other land
rise with the help
of pine

great boulders
round-backed like whales
come up for air
and twenty feet later
plunge back
into the depths

forty-two

we walk up
past the last meadows
the ones
no one plows
any more

we find the perfect hill
to build our
hundredth house

forty-three

these mountains
are about to silence
my voice

I must learn
their alphabet

PART TWO

the stay

one

these are the elements
in my hands
mud from on back
sand from the ravine
golden straw from the side
of the road   mixed
to frame a window

everything else waits
novels   acrylics
the Viennese waltz
in February's vein

these are the facts   I carry
a gun next to my rib cage
the not so imaginary Cain
living nearby might come
looking for me   I die by
turns and he   he falls

when the sun shines it's all right

I work in a world out of reach

my mother at ninety-three

still sews humming

songs from the Thirties

waiting this long to see me

win   and I with a broken toe

can't tell her where I stand   it's

this business of being

gloriously lost   like

the tarantula that came out of the wall

before I mudded the cracks   it

was walking sideways in the grass

in the hallucinatory green

of the earth   its velvet dress leery

in the wind

two

who will house my paintings
or sell color to a world of black
and white?   the answer is the world's
affair   how the momentary eye
dislikes an empty wall

there is urgency to the nervous system
a wanting to lend toys an air
of seriousness   a formula
for both survival and vision
how the politics of light
can suffer multitudes

I make mistakes   falter on the rendering
of a pony   one of its legs doesn't seem
to fit under it   so I begin again

the foal mistakes its dying
for the morning   once more
all is milk and mist

one rides past childhood now
collecting shadows   shadows
of a ladybug nurse to a moon
sitting on its empty saddle
sugar shadows of the hummingbird
painted on the white ribs
of the moonlight

<u>three</u>

the new cat came
in the arms of the town drunk
we don't want a cat   I said
your wife sends it
he said

smiling
the way I like him best
when he's not sober

are we clouds
if we pass?   I ask him

he comes into the house
to explain   how the cat
kept flirting with her
up a ways   where Redford's
filmmakers have attracted
so many cars she thought
the animal would be killed

I offer him a drink
things are not bottled up
between us   are they?
he asks

<u>four</u>

the Sunday morning odor
of sanctimonious words
comes from the Presbyterian
church   bread from that small
oven of dogma   I keep my own
counsel   pruning this or that
branch of excellence
from a corral of galaxies

in that not so imaginary orchard
muffled by infinities of moss
I harvest one planet at a time
each examined so they don't carry
worms from death to rainbow

I borrow mostly what is absent
a moon that circles the mind
a cosmos about to jump-start
from a cloggd artery
this earth is petal of a long

goodbye   I'll be hers

when I am dust   pollen

carried to the hive

a sprig of lilac grafted

to the month of May

<u>five</u>

when I think I have met
the oldest man   I meet yet
another   this one tottering
that one blaming his wife's skirts
literally keeping his gravestone
cooling

they walk toward me   they wave
from cars driven by that other lady
I am leaning on my shovel
and they go by laughing
having gone from bad
to worse on a day's
notice

they build nothing
they have stopped what started
with drinking early

one of them walks

in circles   this gives him
something to do
at ground zero

it's like that here   a kingdom
of dissolute humor where
the impossible is something
with a touch
of Spanish madness
as when old man Padilla
wants back a tool
he never lent me

six

on the other hand the young ones
come to rebuild my house   they
come in droves   spit and piss
needing money for booze
if no wife is home to claim it first

from them I learn bargains
are agreed upon with a conviction
that ends when they overdose
three days before the preacher
preaches them dead

this is my illegitimate brood
blessing and disaster
in the midst of so much sunlight
I want their lives to go light
but sunshine is only paint
it looks good on a wall
when the painter is around

each night   or one of these deaths
has the feel of the sinister forest
where the Egyptian eyes
on the trunks of the aspen
never blink

this passage as into wax   this
station between life and death
in unlabelled bottles contains them
as if they were grasshoppers
childish gods have set to jumping
from one coffin to another
their finished lives choking
the sides of the roads with
white wooden crosses

seven

the attic became
a bedroom for bent heads
where the aria of the rain
that baritone   drowns
in its own applause

under the staircase we placed
brooms and wine and dust
hiding its dancing histories
upright

life is short
it is the color of eggshell
we only have time
to brew good tea
and have its odor
permeate the books
caressed with reading
history   the form this nation
took into an attic   Whitman's

lilacs next to Lincoln

a Los Angeles with no freeways yet

a broom to sweep America

under the rug   but dream her

well into the future

eight

bygone worlds return to the brain
morose with echoes   but how
does one get rid of the remora
feeding upstream on heartbreak?

coffee-splattered letters
go yellow in one's hands
yesterday develops stains
like bullet holes   pianos
hounded by broken hands
forgotten voices heading
north with the albatross

or that travel with us a ways
to sink under seasons of nostalgia
until one's friends accumulate
on the other shore   who laugh
without our hearing them
unable to believe

and sometimes   as in a film

one sees a city singing against time

the unpainted house where one

no longer lives   and all one can do

is hoard the silence that made

the roar go deaf

<u>nine</u>

recognize it?   it's
your own body's time
your mind's coming
extinction   your spirit's
immense release

what an irony
to have the flesh go bad
when the flashes are
the greatest

but we're premature
it's just that now one knows
the grave is where
four by eight
eight feet down you lie
for sure before your time

and it may be larger
than that   a door

we take for granted

a handle we turn

fearing the unknown

let's celebrate knowing more

that we know less because

less is more   look

we wear black   the Chinese

white   who on earth

can be mourned with confidence?

<u>ten</u>

here the cemeteries plunge
down the mountain   one
is sure to be buried
standing for rigor mortis

if you are a member
of this or that clan
you'll have a mention
in the paper   a plot
a grave full of plastic flowers
below the open beak
of the Sangres *

those who can afford it
celebrate dying with
taffeta skirts
the lips of lilies

the poor get buried
in some socket

of ignorance

ignorant until the last minute

when they let out a scream

it's such an odd thing to die

when you have given birth

to so much that you forgot

to place under the mattress

*The range named the Sangre de Cristo Mountains

eleven

those geraniums
fool no one   this is a town
where all the curtains
have them looking at each
other   staring
across an empty street
full of dogs   drunks
on crutches   oh

when the stranger comes
and he's new   like an angel
or a toy   the paisley
shivers   the breeze
dials gossip green
old cronies laugh

the stranger's here
to be devoured   look
at him   birds of darkness
see him beginning to dissolve

in your auspicious gullets

let him taste you also
let him get back at you
from his window   let him
destroy you with his
distant thunder   his pride
in having crawled up your wall
like a beetle

<u>twelve</u>

here's the stranger's byline
submitted before posthumous
corrections   first

you should have a full description
of his vanilla childhood throne
rattled by the stormy weather
of the Atlantic   then
the usual number of abbots
refuted priests and arid malcontents
kissing his ring   possible women
wrestling him to the floor
the magnificent way he has
of pretending his truth
will reckon with the end

he wears the monkey down
and cracks all syntax open
 eventually the teratoid sea

swallows him and agrees
with its dim light to be his brain

the aleph bursts from quartz
spontaneity from abandon
a great false ease appears to
succotash him till he's born
again   leaping out of
October's yellow mantle
a pope that can shit in the forest

thirteen

Pythagoras' mouth is full
of nails   and with summer's
warmth his damsel branches
climb   dancing with each rung
of yellow pine

fellows mired in expletives
caress the walls with a clay hand
twelve hundred new muscles
turn popular   building
is a snap if the captain can doze
at noon in the broom closet

the watery light of August
lends house-building
a cave dweller's tropical
confidence   latitude

all dream must mate with sleep
Baudelaire downs the grey sea

after a binge   service the future

he says   getting his legs

out of the way of the Titanic

<u>fourteen</u>

over the peaks
constantly hovering
Venus burns her diamond
past the Jemez Range   Arizona
is where the light is pink
and then a lengthy corpse

in fields here scattered horses
neigh   a dog pisses against
a final stone   all one can see
turns black

the tender blue has said goodbye
the world was that something
of desire wounds a million persons
in a planet lurching sideways   all of us

are ready and willing but now
time has come to rest   all
of us want warmth beneath

a mother's blanket

can you hear that distant humming?
someone is baking bread somewhere
Wolfgang's music is being played
without its codas   dawn has yet to sniff
the distant odor of a skunk

fifteen

the beams that support his house
were virgins in the forest once

if not   the stove will enlist
the inherent flame that was to rot
on the ice-shattered flank
of the mountain

thieves   mere boys   knock
on the door at night   they
show me an extension cord
they want to sell   sell cheap
promising it hasn't been stolen yet

soap   liquor   nervous books
borrowed time's at work on paper
prodded by angels of greed

he said   and I quote him
verbatim   if property is theft

then theft is property

and the gods smile   they
find money ludicrous
a single carpenter ant
can perforate kingdoms
from within   be thieving

they say at heart   be willing
to clean bedpans and have sex
whenever   but cut your hands off
before you allow the manacles
of prayer to encircle your wrists

sixteen

in back of our half acre
by the brook that elbows into fields
thirst cracks the ground open
a single apple tree has gone ignored
unpruned for decades

this year it bore two apples
taste of the golden times
when the villagers ground
their corn under its shade

I climbed it
in my arms
to trim the sky
above it   wanting
its wedding dress
to come to life
when spring
arrives with its bees
to let the sunlight riot

from within   as we

ourselves must do

seventeen

I dreamt my father died again
dreamt of thirty Christs
whose sanity could not abide
galaxy or sparrow

I call on the angels of the seesaw
to come and see how with humans
thoughts expand in all directions
how they sit with the moonlight
on the horns of mythic beasts

I saw how I was coming
when I went   my ancestors
were probably about   it isn't easy
to drown a child without a crone
that tells you funny stories

I wait each day for proof
and only see that grass can sprout
out of a gravestone

if graves don't yield the dead

and the dead are silent   then

what has been said of life

is right   that it is real because

it happens to be dream

eighteen

we brought Machita once to visit here
she confronted a bull belonging
to a Martinez   and went back
to Minnesota   proud and playful
medals on her didactic chest of love

button of a nose   she
was a bulldog connected
to the Almighty   a mischievous
megaton   four legs supporting
the luxury of herself   always
chosen for a walk   a disdainer
of inferior hydrants   mother
of eight   with just one casualty

I delivered the wet and wrinkled
things and kept Popo   the brightest
till one day   over nothing
over a meal she was served
after a minor surgery   she died

the school of veterinary medicine at
the university was to blame   incompetents
fed her when they shouldn't have   oh
so sorry   so surprised

I went to see her at the morgue
the unfinished   the darling   the
absent   stiff by then   unmoving   gone
all I could touch was the stuffing
that had housed her game

nineteen

we came on stilts of light
leaping from one sunset
to the next   thinking that citizens
were expected to glow

then it got dark
as only dark can get
the stars were thumbprints
pinning us down
to steps of red clay

weeds trembled
because the sky
was never there
it was up   up

we learned new words
we said *chamisa*
the thing got wise
went yellow

with yellow blossoms

a year has gone by
it's too painful to speak
of having had
a previous home

a storm of ochres
obscures that issue
the lemon light
has asked us to go blue
with the silence
and the summer dust
of the crossroads

<u>twenty</u>

they farmed beans among
unyielding rock in the upper
meadows where at noon
wild turkeys call   the earth was
young   Delfino still alive

the Los Alamos atom brought
jobs and notions   the priest
was sent for a twelve pack
perfect

the ancient grannies
who sat in their doorways
puffing at lavender ecstasy
were replaced by mirrors
custom is to have a hacking
cough   loud and insistent

what was right   the wall-bending
families among pigs and goats

gone the way of the fix

hardly a rooster crows
even the cows are dishonest
money came   the wars went
burning the wedding photos

distrust dwells at the edge
of politeness   only the very old
the tottering blind like a burning
can show you on godlike shoulders
where the furrows went

to go to church
one pries open
the legs of the prostitute

<u>twenty-one</u>

once in a while
a stone
falling
will lecture
a ravine

once in a long while
a raven
will impersonate
silence
with a call

but it takes
a thousand years
for gold rushing
through darkness
to reach the heart
of quartz

meantime

Eliseo waits for the school bus
to bring his daughter home
watching how time
postpones his day

Father Roca gives the boys
who came to Guillermo' funeral
hell for aiding and abetting
the white dust

twenty-two

today water drips from the eaves
with great candor   up the road
past Petronila's house   a tree
full of apples holds up fists of gold
against the steel-grey clouds
seething in the mountains

candy wrappers   beer cans
the road is littered
with what people went by with

drops of gasoline in puddles
play at being peacocks
and as the love of light
wanes into a bit of chill
one cares for it more   the wind
is a caress from a forgotten hand
a hand that pressed yours once
all five musicians

doña Margarita comes out
of her house across the street
to shake her tablecloth and share
a few crumbs with the sparrows
her former husband   two houses up
has asked again for the pick
he never lent me

what does he want with it   I
wonder   picks are dangerous
they can open up the ground
before one's feet

twenty-three

dusk

lullabies
walk homeward now

the world's nectar
piles up west

a girl walks by
her reflection
on the window
adds something
to her body

she's pregnant
or so reveals
the crooked glass

my life is a leaf
blown across the fields

says the Andean song
it knows no solace
it has no future

I cry
and it seems
as if my soul
was singing

twenty-four

a harp
stained my fingers
purple
with its mulberry song

dreams
like linen
wash at dawn

such birds hang from air
as know direction

amazing
to be the young
propellant
of one's heart

once I was
a wounded creature
by the roadside

asleep

to teach myself

to wake

<u>twenty-five</u>

(for Elena)

I am waiting for a call
from your four chambers
daughter of the bottomless
sea   conceived the night
the moon read poems
to an audience about to be
your cosmos

tell me who you are   where to place
your soul   how the heart is going
to make you happy   please call
and let me know if others form
as shadows   for you were a shadow
I placed once on Santa's knee
a child to whisper what you wanted
whether vast or tiny like the strength
of spring   oh   you made that call

you had asked

for your mother's cry
as from a shell
a ram's horn
inside her

I have waited for your maturity
to unfold as melody
waited to hear
you upon the stage of song
banishing the temporary
from the funny eternities
that pour fairytales in one's ears

twenty-six

one brother goes to hit another
from behind over a disputed
piece of land   these are

older men   not hot-headed
youngsters   the violent one
for years a gardener

the quarrel simmers
on the back burner of greed
and years go by   nothing
happens   the two of them
sit having coffee in a café
as if no axe could ever
split a skull in half

another time   perhaps from
boredom or because idiocy
like an elegant snake
raises it head   the issue

is settled violently
their two widows will sell
the land and move in together

necessity is a crutch
that women understand
but their sons are now of an age
that continues to kill

twenty-seven

to water the garden in summer
one opens a sluice in the *acequia*
out in back where the dragonflies
exist on small doses of honey

permission is granted for the water
by the elected water man   the
mayordomo who gives you day
and hour for the water to come
running dusty with success

the peach tree drinks
the pear tree drinks
the plum tree I got
from doña Margarita
as a nearly dry twig
the apple tree from
Española   the lawn
in front of the house

which drinks the most
and settles back to try
growing a beard again

when the job is done
I go back and close the vein

the spurned water turns
seeking a neighbor   it floods
fields full of cow pies
harboring psychedelic
mushrooms in their crust

<u>twenty-eight</u>

ten loads of wood
will keep the kitchen
warm

and as with Europe
with its forests gone
the tongues of flame
will lick the mountain
clean

darkness has prodigious
birthdays
while in the temple
the gods burn
low

one goes
a moth
to light a candle
no one claims

the candle's odor

it is all around us
telling us to paint
the animals we hunt
on a cave wall

<u>twenty-nine</u>

she was playing such syrupy crap
I envied the dead one in his
copper coffin up front

the music was like those pale
tendrils one sees growing
in the basements of humid
prairie homes and it came
from an out-of-tune piano
for twenty Presbyterian
minutes

I would have walked out
except that everyone's familiar
with the heroic nature
of my shyness   it can take
anything before it minces with
assertion   but then

when she stopped   such are

the blessings of God   two

ministers took over and it was

worse   much worse

Scriptures and hell-fire

given more play

than pygmy thunder

from asparagus fingers

so much for the boy dead

from an overdose

who chose   I am sure   a grave

on the edge of the cemetery

so that when no one is looking

he can puncture his arm

on the wire fence

<u>thirty</u>

beyond the trash dumped illegally
where a rocky ground nurses
the skeletons of cows
exposing their white rosaries
a dusty road meanders without
heir

one makes one's way through
piñon trees and past timothy grass
stumble over quartz and mica
reflecting fifty miles of sunset
until one comes upon rocks
the size of silent houses
arranged by the hands
of an absent master

sometimes the wind
cannot be quiet there
it whispers as it sifts
through a piney colander

of needles   that sound
and the lowing of cows far away
the calls of ravens and magpies
is this earth's music

if sometimes small birds add
their cries   you know
you can add yours also

thirty-one

it's getting late   I am
cold   the wild apples shrink
on the branch and look
like old ladies by a mirror
fallen from grace

a box of pears goes bad
a pumpkin must be shelled
so that in spring we can
pin new medals on the chest
of the heroic soil

my hands are sore   grooves
have opened on some fingers
my fingernails feel like shoes
a size too small   they call it

winter   winter's coming
they say

the insect world boils down to
laying eggs   the trees tune in
to the distant rumble of angina
and go yellow   cowards all

the snow has worlds to conquer
its first patrols advance
camouflaged as moths

friend   if you come
bring your unabused breast
the morning smile of your hands
I'll either be at the bus station
or high up that do-you-remember tree
chattering with a capuchin monkey

*****

www.ingramcontent.com/pod-product-compliance
Lightning Source LLC
Chambersburg PA
CBHW060423090426
42734CB00011B/2427